JOSHUA

JOSHUA

by

WILLIAM WALLIS

Stone and Scott, *Publishers*
Sherman Oaks, California

Joshua

First edition 1994

Printed in the United States of America

©1994 by William George Wallis
Photographs by Mitzi Trumbo
Cover Design by Eva Reti

Library of Congress
  Catalogue Number 94-066740

ISBN 0-9627031-5-X

For Leslie,
Joshua's mother and
faithful center of the Wallis family
and for her children
Asher, Joshua, Rachel and Zara

Table of Contents

Illustrations

JOSHUA

POEMS FOR JOSHUA

THE FLIGHT OF HANDS

Your silken hands have finally become tools,
Their grasping now explores, then manipulates
      the coverlet of bamboo prints..
My fingers are examined also,
Great smooth stalks on a vague field
And cursory artifacts from a nascent dimension.
Soon feathering tips will begin their nascent dance
Across my face and along the edge of things
Like tables and the evolving hunch that these
Gargantuans will return when they disappear.
These hands will run quick over cotton fields
Until an urge to fly fills them and they become
      linked extensions of the soul—
Already they linger and hang in the air,
Preparing for soaring flight. Beneath
This need for flight is the growing sense
That seeing is only partial truth.
When we leave your sight, fair ones,
You can trust us to return,
For our flight circles about you now and now,
From this horizon to the next.
We could not love you more.
This will be true as long as hands dance,
Stars burn in the dark blanket above
And there in your eyes—
There, where we begin to explore.

AUTUMN SONNET
(for Joshua)

I neglect the roses before my home,
But they in untamed fullness have forgiven me.
Their dry petals fall from bulb to loam,
As each bloom's design melts into a sea of light.
They do not prove their rooted love for earth,
Or draw back a curtain of words to show
The soul's leisure. The depth of their surface
Is the cloth of sight, cool flakes of the soil's night.
Fascicles of light drift among the stems
And toward me, before my son's tiny hands
Close over my eyes in a petalling veil,
And I must guess who is there behind me.
    Is it the shield and rose of time, my playful
    Responsibility, and the first form of love?

AUTUMN EYE

The roses before the house have blossomed
Three times this Fall. Their fragrance graces
Each entrance of family. Every exit is protected
By a rainbow veil—laughter of the earth.
Out there trees blaze, move swan-like in calm fury,
They will shed their cloaks to mime black lightning's
     rise from soil to cloud.
Dark seasons always penetrate my senses with longing—
As I fall to sleep, wild geese call down from great heights.
Here within, the sheltered rows of books stand fast,
Their leaves chafing gently for the reader's mind.
Children fill the rooms with roles and new text,
Their finest portrayals of giant parents.
     They pass easy out through the light–barbed curtain,
     While my eye, book–bent, lingers on their wings' traces.

ISRAEL
(for Joshua)

Winter slips its dry scales from your second year,
And you and your brother may enter Spring,
Cross the elastic river of consciousness
To a richer land for the self's clay forming.
The chosen ten scouted the promised land
North to Arad, Hebron and Schechem that July.
What will remain in forty years of those places
If we now break God's law, nature's and our own?
In your nascent youth, do you feel the strength
To renew Jerusalem and replace the millions lost?
They cry to you from earth's atomic ovens.
Finding no Moses, no sign, they swirl, lost.
  Spy of my heart! When I fall and see God's face,
    Remember Jerusalem, and replace me.

BROTHERS
(for Asher and Joshua)

Asher lies sprawled, eyes sunk in image, mind
Off where five–year–olds merge color and form.
Joshua studies, then heads straight for him, drawn
Drawn by his brother's careless grace and fast gaze.
Slowly, Asher turns to regard him, sees through
The hazy pre-dawn of his brother's stare
A sign, and with the pure calm of the wounded,
Lifts his head to accept a kiss of pure care.
Then the sweet heads turn to watch as one; my boys
Linger in the sacred space their touch has made,
While I burrow quick through earth marrow
To brothers—mine, my mother's—lost in sorrow.
　　Can the sweet need that drew your lips to grace
　　Calm Cain's stolid rage, flush Abel's pale face?

GRACE

Late arriving, I study
    my sons' sleep:
Asher's moist brow
    rises blind
Searching for my kiss;
    near him,
Joshua sprawls in flight,
    right arm sifting air.
The dark house becomes
    a silken field,
My little wanderers
    breathe light
in the night. Above them
    their mother sleeps;
her dream enclosing
    theirs, for now.
And above that dream,
    dark forms
shift easy, fold into me
    as I climb
finite stairs of grace
    to the only
rest I have known.

JOSHUA'S FLIGHT

Miniature landscape
                    your face
lights — lake eyes
                    luminous
                              as you run
reaching up to me
                    the palms of your hands , cheeks
              one plane
rise to me—

              Strangely
                    you are wingless
trust in flight   —
                    God, gentle in me.

Blessed son
              your sweet weight
                              disappears
as you fly up to me
                              my
                    great hands
                              your wings.
I fear you
              may simply vanish
before I can
              steal back my breath
and steady my poor heart
                    for its return.

LULLABY FOR JOSHUA

Second tiny gift of grace,
    All of heaven's in your face.
In those tiny planets shine
    God's sweet light and pureness fine.
Second tiny gift of grace,
    All God's heaven's in your face.

As the planets circle cold,
    We will not fear growing old.
Others fear that emptiness
    Drifting with no sun's caress.
As the planets circle cold
    We will not fear growing old.

While the stars are in your eyes,
    Lions chill the night with cries.
Galaxies can whirl away,
    Novas, Black Stars tug and play.
Our Universe is in your eyes,
    Ageless fears must run and hide.

Way up in the great somewhere
    Angels sing without a care.
Is the edge of time so near?
    Can our love erase all fear?
Way up in the great somewhere
    Angels sing without a care.

LULLABYE

Wind moves branches   brush trembles
small wings flutter   over bare stone
From the silence   between light and dark
from lost shadows   a thought grows
a voice, soft snake   emerges metallic
from the glowing   thicket's slow dance
winds like incense   over carpet sand.

Where do you fly   little bird?
Whom do you call   little voice?
Answer, answer me   fly and call to me
Breezes, touch earth   with pure tendrils
Clouds above,   wet earth with your tears.

Hear the song   that winds before you
leading you   where you may follow
Seek its wisps   deep in the forest
In the plain   on the mountain top
You dream   a silver bird hides in the clouds.

Again you dream   a magical beast
sings deep in   the clouded forest
but you will   never find it
it will always   be before you
singing in soft   breezes always
just before you   secret, moving quick.

Breeze through branch   shadow over stone
Small silent motions   linger, answer.

WOLVES

This house's memory is free of time;
Its wooden bones do not remember trees.
This family's soul grows in wild freedom.

When at night we several lie united
By breath and little tugs of thought,
We signal each other with long calls

As we lie falling toward memories
Of when I held my two cubs in my arms
And before our wooden cage

We howled together as the great
Pitted sphere rose from the sycamores
Along South Stanley Avenue.

Cicero said,	Descartes re-
Contemplation	turned to zero
of the uni–	to be sure he was
verse liberates.	free from error.

In the fierce energy of day, my boys,
Two and six, signal their brotherhood
With scat—screamed out, then cooed.

In wild patterns of chase and dance,
They free themselves from my need
To piece together the fragments they scatter,

They resist my need to trace
Their disappearing fontanels into
The perfect egg shells of their future.

ECHO

At ten months my little Joshua sings
The endless song every child utters from birth,
When breath slipped in to bring first wince and sigh,
And turgid lungs repelled the sea for earthly air.

He cries for hunger, gurgles at breast,
Coos at cuddling, whooshes at stun and fall,
Each a stutter-step in the evolution of speech
From hunger's snap to the whine for all.

Now we sit face to face and he forms wide-eyed
Four hollow clicks. Abrupt, my breath catches.
He eyes my mask. Does he also hear the far
Doors of rail cars and chambers slam shut?

Does he see in the vast, bolted room of my eye
The hands of history's clock crush millions,
Their breath and songs consumed? He listens
As swirls of infant cries circle above us.

They sigh dark songs of thanks for you, Joshua—
Angel without wings, singer without art.
Listen and raise your voice to those whose place
In this passing play you will assume
          as iron curtains part.

CONCERT

All concrete thought can be traced
To one in a series of images
The mind catches that cling to memory
Like a child to a galloping mare.
It was an evening concert, when we
Lay together in your small bed,
And I sang you toward sleep
With ballads, arias, *Lieder.*
When the words were English,
You played nearby at your ease,
But with Schubert, you ceased play,
Came, and hovered over me,
And with your steady hands
Studied my singer's mask.
      Ruh'n in Frieden, alle Seelen.
In simple gestures, you stroked my cheeks
And lips as I formed sounds
      foreign to you—
Sounds like great engines,
And the black blur that
Disappears under the fast car,
The muffled scream
In the rear view mirror—
Yet your hands are calm, steady.
In your trusting search of
The unknown in me, I see that
I have driven Death far away.
Your clear eyes make
Inconsequent any power
      in the face of love.

How can you know that bright shadow?
There is love, not fear,
In your near countenance.
I rise and go, leave
You to your memories and dreams.
I close the door softly.
Death, too familiar to fear,
Can not erase the delicate trace
Of your hand's memory of my face.

RETURN

When he returns to his parents' bed
To snuggle warm and fragrant as a fawn,
What is there then in the universe
But the seashell curve of his ear
(Labyrinthine in receding balance and sheen),
The bright isle of his horizon eye
Gazing over the range of rough blankets,
The soft sour swirl of his early breath
    filling this new world.
To the spareness of his shared design,
His playful sounds and words,
The simplicity of his discoveries
I offer my song of praise,
This dear play of the mind,
All that will remain of these hands
Now grown fond of making children and beds.

JANUARY 5, 1994
On the Event of Naming Joshua's Sisters,
Rachel and Zara)

What pleasure to sing the praises of infants,
Whose form is an angel without wings,
Whose songs teach us unconditional love,
Whose face is a mirror of the generations,
Whose eyes see all things but remember little,
Whose pain is quick and vanishing,
Whose need is our reward,
Whose cries wake us in the night, whose pale
    face shames the cold moon.
Whose little kicks break walls of seriousness;
Who suffer our clumsiness with adoration,
Who redefine gravity with lightness,
Who expand the universe with sweetness and warmth,
Whose invisible wings will raise them one day
    to recreate themselves.

MAN RUSHING

The old man rushes across the street, his cane
Furious and clacking in front of his bent
Torso leaning, stiff arms, jagged neck and knees.
I swerve my car to miss him, without checking
If anyone is beside me. He never raises his head.
In the rearview, his curious glance burns
At my failure. And all day long I've thought
Of little but my sons and their need for me now.
What would you do, silent father, now that you
Have fallen under the cars you built?
Shall I continue to fill these empty frames
For my children to build on, if they choose?
    Where am I rushing, when the truth is home
    Resting calm in the beds of my Asher and Josh.

TANKA FOR JOSHUA

Green stains the ends of
branches, look down and
you'll find green of grass
if you look carefully, if
you look carefully, you'll see

in summer the limbs
spread heavy over grass and
abandoned grass grows thick
down there, under dark limbs
you can sleep on that cool sheet

in autumn leaves are
scarce and strange fruit lie heavy
on grass, beneath trees
they wait, as air thin with cold
winds about the thick dark trunks
hunting for green, like you

LOST SONNET

In my most perverse dream I awake
As in an earthquake, struggling against
Unseen forces to rise, steady myself,
Finally descend sudden stairs littered with books.
In the kitchen, where glacier stillness reigns,
I begin to sense they're all gone, my little doves.
But even so I search the pantry, cabinets,
The refrig, the sink, and call for them to come,
As if this kitchen were not a graveyard.
Again, finally, I go to the infants' room
And find not even a little ash in the cradles there,
I rush to my boys' rooms, speak in subdued tones
    With their toys and books. My wife's footprints
    Are everywhere I go. I circle in them.

JOSHUA AT FOUR
(for Los Angeles)

Deep in the City of Los Angeles ,
A house—built of wood, in 1927—
Stands behind a rail fence, now a barricade
Piled fragrant with roses, red wounding green.
I patrol the front and my pocket knife darts
Into the thicket to trim faded blooms,
While my Joshy trails me, critical and grave:
Not that one, little Daddy, it's still good.
When he was two, I crushed him in my arms here
(And brushed his face with a great crimson rose).
At three, he peeked giggling through these vines.
I warned, *Be careful of the thorns—they sting.*
And he called out, *Be careful of the roses—they sing.*

       City of rough surfaces, remember the roses among
       The thorns: Angels still sing behind your barriers.

ASHER AND JOSHUA, AUTUMN 1993

JUNE 19, 1994

Between your age and mine, the whispered movements—
Delicate, wave-like, like daddy-long-legged
Mosquito hunters in the sun-filled farm shed
Where I hurled myself and lay far from your voice—
Have weakened, dissipating love and pain,
And the essential combination of them
You create in me—you, the restless need
I will not accept as Fate, Old Shadow of mine.
But some answers grow from within my own skull
As nights I lie down to dream again in your skin:
The curtains of time burn quick and I once more see the world
From your vast shoulders and may at last kiss your scarred hands..
    You call to me over all those long years,
    And I murmur Yes, and dry my son's tears.

PSALMS

1

Master of particles and the expanding universe,
Author of original chaos and pattern,
Lord of furious energy, of plotless
Cords of ineluctable force,

Hear the piping song and dancing rhythms
I lift up to you amidst the heavy smoke
Of this century—beside which all
Previous ages will appear harmless.
As the ancients lifted to You
Dance of ram and unbridled aria
Master, hear my prayer.

You, who opens the inner eye to
The diaphanous expanse of questioning,
The trap of paradox;
At the same time You create
The centripetal concepts
That hurtle us inward to You,
Bind my soul to You.

Do You wait beyond gravity,
Beyond intellect, will and emotion,
In blinding light or beyond concept,
In the darkness before thought,
In thought's existential shadows
lingering in dimensionless pre-light?

Will You burn clear my critical mind
After the empty search?
You are all things.
Are these your flames then?
Can we know these flames as signs,
But still not see them,
Blinded as we are by clouds?

All-encompassing God of exaltation and doubt,
You who know my sin,
My unstable center,
Yet does not crush me
Beneath Your unbound power.
Hear the flames singing
The cries of the raped and tortured,
The slanted face of the loved adult
        above the abused child,
The addicted newborn,
The bloated infant of Africa,
The chemically maimed,
The genetically insane —
The crushed skulls of ancient Africa,
The crushed skulls of Biko's Africa.
Hear my song of pain.

Hear the cries of those who like so many cattle
Are driven from place to place,
from field to army,
to battle, to Sheol—

They wait silent, then cry out.
Pinned, they flutter hard
Under the vast night's space,
Pierced through with the stars'
        ancient light.

Help me, Master,
To the freedom
To see the pain
And fight its rebirth.
It is my struggle.
Yet so much seems
Formulated against me.

And for the swirling questions
In my son's pure eyes
And the sweet piping
He lifts up to you
Through the writhing elements,
Thank you, Master.

2

O God, how majestic is Your evening sky,
The gold and crimson weave of Your aery mantle
Above the cloud-brushed western expanse.
The dome of darkening blue is awash
With purple fleece and thunder song.
The wind's great wing sweeps eastward toward morning.
Beneath this star-pierced map of an exploding
        collapsing universe,
This great layered growth of time and matter
Sketched for the earthbound
In only the cold words of science—
And veiled in the shroud
Of cosmic or atomic distance.
Far beneath you, I dream
Of eternity's arched skull
And its shifting motions,
I study its protean forms and movement
Above the mountain's press
Against the earth crust.
My eyes strain to fix the vast swirl,
The numberless movements
Above the clouds ,
As stars emerge—your
Flickering signature of first fire,
Each spark relative to another time,
Each little time clock swarming above
In the distant froth of unbound energy.
Will my inner eye see
What fails these spheres?
Will You reach to me

Through the uncircumscribed maelstrom of old chaos,
Through the arcing dance of elements,
Through the tunnel of thought's spidery expanse,
Through the cyclotron's exponential particle speeds,
Through the sliding onion layers of time wrapped about us
That contain the gradual expanse of galaxies and worlds,
Supporting a collapsing vision of order.
Dancer of the particles' dance,
Of wave and electron field,
Draw my soul to thy inner circles,
Into the gears of the vast watch
We construe and will unwind.
Make my song a mirror of pleasing forms.
Only let me survive the eternity of doubt
Winnowed from countless wars,
From torture and cruel guilt,
From those who have all the answers
Yet rage ineffective against evil.
Protect us from the hatred
Evoked by gods of the earth who
Destroy the innocent,
Corrupt the good,
Hurl the bolt / the final
Breath / drawn in horror.
Is this fretted expanse your consciousness, Lord?
Do you feel my heartbeat's ripple,
The Monarch flutter of my soul,
In the vast oceans where you anchor?
Who is honored in your presence more,
He who accepts or questions?

Are my questions anathema?
Am I wrong to see a new wilderness
In this land of unbearable riches?
With all this matter between You and me,
Oldest friend and eternal guide,
Who can blame this singer's
Longing for a sign? Only
A simple star with light undying,
The cool tug of gravity reversed,
A circular dance of your signature above us
In this starry, flooding night.
Lord of space and time, Bring peace
To the forked creatures of Your earth
That we may write your name in the cold heavens
We now study as mere fire and artless flow.
Yet I know that as the soul is suffused throughout the flesh,
You are somehow here everywhere.
Cool is the wind sweeping down now
From the mountains to the north
And from your interstellar castle
Of pure line and point.
Lord of river slide and sea shift,
And the earth's ride about a darkening sun,
Accept my restless soul,
And those of my father, my mother,
My sons and daughters, and beloved wife
Into the vast ocean of your burning night,
The dark eternal space hovering
Between thought and action.

3

Teacher of prayer and inner calm,
Still point in the turning universe,
Teach me patience for false teachers,
For sophists and demagogues
Who crush You with lies.
Teach me to pray for those
Who cut at my soul with steel words
Who sneer that my beliefs are banality,
Whose politics has replaced You in their heart and mind,
Who glorify the physical, deny the spirit,
Who take from the poor in their wealth,
Who abuse their education
And throw blindness into the crystal eyes of the young,
Who lie in wait for the innocent.
You snakes and scavengers whose laughter
Defeats the gentle of spirit.
What forces shaped these spiders
That clog learning's flow with their webs:
Twisters of spirit and goodness,
Monsters of history's slaughter and sickness,
Shapers of this century, a violent nightmare.

   Shoah, Shoah, Shoah.

How shall I believe that you could have existed
In our time, in a time where I lived and loved
And counted and still count the vast numbers
      of those lost to the air?
Shall I say that evil walked the earth?

Yet they too die,
Fall back beside the pure they have burned.

The atmosphere is thick with holy ashes

The healthy they have sickened,
The naive they have crushed.

You mockers, you will know in those darkening moments,
The dead weight of your brackish heart's writhing
In the mud of your mind's last clutching gesture,
The mind's dissolution to blood,
The mouth's dry gasp,
The lung's solid earthiness,
The echoes of false, false words
As they drag you down to
To where there are no more games
And the last crushing truth of your lies will
Savage the last millisecond before you
Twist back into the tunneling light
Where they all await you?

And do your victims there embrace you?
Do you shed your reptilian ethos
And see with the eyes of children?
Can we who remain behind believe this
And be cleansed of our earthly hatred and guilt?

Or will you writhe as we might wish
In the empty dungeon you created
When your consciousness had cause?
If I could create an afterlife for you—
You evil who knowledgeably enjoy your evil—
I would allow you in that instant,
In that extreme freedom of death,
To create from the remnants of your lies
A desired place to hover for eternity.
This would be my prayer: that your will
Should extend to the very end of your time.

May God speak to us all
As he spoke to Moses.
May he purge me of my fear and hate.

4

The universe collapses
When a child is torn from life.

Words for lost children fall,
Drift from clinging furrow to thorn,
Rattle through ditches and culverts to
To rest in chthonic neighborhood drains
Near the school yard where
Piping voices lingered too long.
Drifted from vast school yards,
Climbed trusting into the maw of a smiling car,
Were rushed to candied silence down
Breathless roads without end.

Trustless, shifting
Words wander into dreamfields,
Sorrowing, sickened
Words fall into white spaces,
Between the radio's scream
The engine whine, the
White, white wind.
Ah, lost sounds:
        fly song
        ant cry
        clay murmur.

Stochastic signs and symbols
Crumble dry from Kronos' lips:
Here a dusty scrap, there a digit

38

Urges from his reptilian past
Writhe where skull buckles spine.
He guides his car by the school.
There beside the drifting entelechy
Is the dry field where
The man-monster crouches
Devouring his litter
Under skies of stone and iron.

For little arms reaching up
To false hands beneath the endless
Green lights of the adult world,
For new souls who sing and
Skip before a crouched beast.
For the weak of the litter,

Whose numbed flesh forms
        milk carton reproductions,
        resident mailings
Fall
        drift
Cathode ray pleas rattle,
                                    rest
On sweet lost eyes and lips
There among the weeds.

Protector and Lord of the Universe,
Remember them,
Brush the soil from those petal cheeks,
As I kiss these words to page.

5

For the homeless
Who writhe in the womb of America
    under steel skies,
Who rushed to the gates of cities
    to sleep on the grates of cities
    and read advertisements with longing,
Who are little signs of Sheol.

Hear the prayers of those
Whose souls burn out under crusted eyebrows,
    bodies shielded by filthy layers
    of gay plastic and gray news sheets,
Who are tortured by the seasons,
    Burned by Summer,
    Mocked by Fall,
    Narrowed by Winter,
    Tortured by Spring—
Crushed by the differences
    marking pleasure for the free,
Who know only the alley, the bench, the crate,
The hopper where the infant was crying out,
    the child sleeping warm found
    by the garbage collector,
The box that sways leeward, then windward, dreaming.
Who know the reality of
The molten toothache grown inward,
Diseases of the Middle Ages,
The endless cough,

The sweetness of decaying food,
    cloth, manners, flesh.

For the homeless
Who descended into the iron hulls for transport and trial,
Who designed escape from invisible boxes
    with dance,
    with instruments of love and death,
Who were born too strong or too weak,
    too beautiful or ugly,
    rich or poor,
    for the family, the neighborhood, the city, the nation.

For those whose visions grace the city
Of concrete sheets and thicket nights
With golden chariots,
The eyes of their wheels glowing amber,
Curbed above the drunk
Lying below.
City of taxis and condoms,
Condominiums and cats,
Home to the homeless
And full of their emptiness.

For those for whom society once made allowance
    but now reviles,
For those children among them,
And for the Brothers and Sisters,
Mothers and Fathers, Lovers and Friends,

Enemies,
Hear my prayer.

For those who went to war and came back fragments,
Deafened by explosive silence,
Blind with unspeakable visions,
Released from cages guarded by beasts
    to cages of freedom,
Abused while pure, filled with fury at nothing—
    at sudden noise, at silence—
Hear my prayer.

For those born to light without a mirror,
Those whose core crumbled and reformed unwhole,
Those who fuse too easily,
Those who cannot interface,
Those who will not bare their soul,
Hear my prayer.

For those who died or went mad,
Tore out their faith by the root
    and scattered it to the four winds,
Or returned to the cave
From the false light of hell they saw
    in the jungles of Asia, or
    in these jungles of steel and stone.

Hear their cries as loud blasts, Lord.
Release them from their torment,
Those who crawl as mice, as ants

Over the concrete and plastic earth.

Allow for our failures
As we reap the corners of our fields,
Fail to repent with whole hearts,
Cease our prayers,
Act no more with charity
By the brackish rivers of our land.

Hear the prayer
Of my homeless soul.

SHABBAT SHUVAH

These words of reflection, regret and renewal
Are for the greater mirror, for all those
I have touched this year with flesh, word or thought.
In a weave of professional and inner
Strands, the tapestry of the year
Was woven with more happiness than regret,
More patience than trial, more love than hate.
Not every year has left me so fortunate.

In the work place I think too much of self:
My need to grow; My hunger for recognition,
And not enough of my students' progress and needs.
I am impatient with colleagues who seem
To know it all but don't produce, others
Who produce nothing but sing of everything they do,
Others who simply exist, marking time
While I see education and society unwind.

When I judge and condemn others
In arrogance, without knowing their wrestling,
When I steal their dignity, their buried passion
Without knowing their dark nights and private terrors,
When I don't find time to listen for the hesitant step,
The door softly closed, the whispered Good-night,
Then I am the last to know their real worth
And should strive to earn their respect and patience.

My family has taught me to love, to finally
Move from passion to compassion and back.
Still, I afflict them with my pain, the unresolved
Nightmares of a blind child crying in the night.
I yell at them, as well as at the man in the mirror,
I project my ambition and tastes on them,
Desire more for them than I am capable
Of giving, more from them than they can give.

But even so, their patience with me is sweet
As honied pages, their pleasant buzzing at
My homecoming will always draw me home to them.
As my colleagues humor me and draw me out,
My family fills me with story and song
And my sleepless nights with dreams of rebirth.
Colleagues and friends fill life with mirth,
Family with dreams, with the chance of self-worth.

But I cannot ask others to do my own work:
They can't know and love what I do not reveal.
Sometimes I think I invent difficulties: I used to think
Trouble followed me, but now realize it's me in pursuit.
This tendency to see the darker side
And let it threaten my peace is cruel
To those near me. I lose patience,
Am seized by old blindness, strike out with words.

So, in the small hours of morning when I walk restless
Through the dark rooms of our house, possessed by
Past numbers and past figures, and long
    for something more,
I open the window on an sea of roses
Shimmering with moon before our house
And feel our little ones swimming the night
Away in dream, dolphins diving deep to translate
The dance of flowers into the mysterious currents
    of their depths.

Is there any truth in this shifting surface of light
Called reality? Who are you? I am a teacher
Of what I love, and one who knows it is not enough
To impart the essential characteristics of the discipline
But somehow to inspire the individual soul
To joy in learning and sharing. I want to describe
A kind of love of the mind to my students, one
That embraces the necessary tensions and resolutions.

My wife and children are the best teachers; they know
That the child inside never stops reaching out for love
And reminding us that we could do more, could speak out
The love and yearning hiding in our hearts, without
Fear of burdening others, simply to celebrate
The desires God has placed deep in our bones.
So many old faces within me cry out,
We could have done more, we could have trusted love!

Still, the teacher learns, as the child fought and fights back
With the help of kind souls. My own children
Embrace the dark child in me and our spirits mix,
To heal my old wounds. My wife and partner has settled
My dreams in her life and lets my ambitions live
At her expense. In the last breath of our life
Together I want nothing more than her hand in mine
And the safe breath of our children near us.

I give to the needy, I could give more.
I love many, I could love them better.
How can we better heal each other?
Let me offer this gift of words, of song
To you, my sisters and brothers, and especially
To children. To the waking, I wish good works
And words to better their lives. To those
Asleep or approaching sleep I offer these words.

When the day has tired me, my endless longing
Joins the starry night like a child's final song.
Hands, forget action; temples, release thought.
All my senses spin, seek sleep's stillness, rest—
And the unobserved soul longs to circle free, search
Deep in night's final expanse for thousandfold life.
From those I have hurt I ask forgiveness,
From those I love I ask patience.
From the past I ask for future strength
To wrestle on with the dark figures that crouch
    by the door of life.

And I thank God for those moments
When I, most fortunate of men,
Pause among the beauties of my home —
Feel its unchanging qualities of light
Enter me, hollow out my bones,
Prepare me for flight.

Rosh Hashanah

Final Thoughts and New Beginnings

EREV ROSH HASHANAH

To this still valley, with its whispered streams
Of wishes and prayer, we have descended.
We have fallen slowly from frigid heights
To twist between the highest windswept peaks
Where the wind's knife makes clear the thin mantel
Of our reality. And now we are in a frigid place
Where the earth beneath us groans ,
The sun and moon are one light,
And horns shiver and moan in gleaming song.
Can we hear the sick, hungry millions from here?
We join in prayer, our vices momentarily,
Less real for a moment for some few—our fears
Perhaps no longer our own, but somehow
Less heavy on our eyes for a moment.
And, even if our prayers rise
To join all the pain prayed out in ages
Of wrath and murderous rage,
Where shall we gather the strength to ask,
How shall we answer for this?

Answers hide themselves among us
In friends, in safe colleagues frozen near,
In random moments collected now in the valley,
In personal investments lost and recollected now—
Like paintings sold too cheaply—
As we strive to construct a chain of thought
Or resolution of lost hope approximating
        an imagined peace . . . .
And as from an autumnal play ground,

Ellen's sweet voice wings among
These proud cedars of Los Angeles
Searching for lowly hyssop.

She hovers above us like a silver dove
Asking, *How shall we answer for this?*
And my child-heart soars to its old pain,
Then returns empty to its cage,
Answerless, silent in despair,
Knowing words are not enough,
Acts are not enough,
The soul must reach out—
Prophet-like, burning with need for God's touch–
To the Other, to consider, to reconsider
The question echoing down
From the mountains of our arrogance
Through the valley of our blind need,
How shall we answer for this?

ROSH HASHANAH

I will pass before You, my wandering not done
And, though many my age have gone on,
I do not think I will die today—
Though the thought becomes less strange
With every day I move from face to face
Among the countless I do not know.
High school and university friends
Have died of cancer, bitter hate, broken hearts.
I go on, like a beast prowling outside camp.

Will the crippled wolf also know peace?

How shall we know peace when the leaders
Before us deny Your presence, leaving
Only gold and success to gage Your light?

Where are You, reliever of hatred and oppression?
You remember the fathomless depths of space
The formless stirrings of creation
From which you shaped us.
Surely You know that that first dark flame
Is still writhing within us as we attempt
To recreate Your urge with our towers
Of limited information and obscene
Power, of inner circles closing in on
Shutting out dreams and imagination,
And You must see how we struggle
With our inner darkness of greed and fear.
Nothing is hidden from You,
As we retreat into these empty rituals;
Nothing is hidden from You:
Our empty suits, empty robes,
Empty words echoing down
From empty worlds within.
How can we be empty
When the near distant world
Is so full of horror and stunning hatred?
Remember Shoah / the machinery of despair,
Stalin's purges / the death of thirty million,
The killing fields of Cambodia / pyramids of skulls,

Bosnia / the warfare of rape,
Ruwanda / machetes in the school yard.

Shoah   Shoah   Shoah

If this little distance makes us helpless,
How shall we fly to you

Over the immeasurable void of space
      separating us?

Will Your words emerge luminous
From the dark lava within me
To answer my prayer for peace?
I ask too many questions,
Lack faith—
Still I cleave to Thee,
Great Mountain of forests and streams
      in the wasteland..

YOM KIPPUR

The evil done is not here,
Simpering and whispering its way
Through a dozen offices and contracts and lies
To slump in a corner or by the door,
Estranged from goodness but leering
Far enough away so we can usually forget it
And silenc e its sick little voice in us.
We groan comically—

Our sated ears record it—
And the sick child we nurse within us
Retreats like a one-legged sparrow
From this glittering pomp and forced service.
Somewhere we began to forget
That it is not only the good deed we do,
But our ability to discern whether
        the deed is good.

I am sick of the self–worship
that has replaced You, Mighty Vision.
I believe You are real, solid as a still voice,
Still as true breath, meditation and song,
Firm as the evening star,
Eternal as children's play and adult terror.
You are there not machine,
Not contractual and not that
Which we can understand.
We can only know You.
And in our longing for entrance
Into the cold circle
Whose dance is always nearly done,
We have forgotten what we need.
Forgive our lies and blindness.
We are blind liars.
Forgive the deepest lie,
The arrogance we so love
In our pursuit of earthly power.

Rock among plastic and concrete,

Let your dew never evaporate
From the ruins of cities.
Straighten this twisted generation
Whose hands are weapons
Whose world is hype
Whose day is night.
We repay you
By eating our own.
The last boundary is broken,
The eye–core has been opened

In a special operation we did not intend,
And an image we no longer
Recognize lives there within us,
Writhing and endlessly falling..
Where is compassion now?
The center is not holding,
The center is changing,
The center is empty.
You are there—this I know, O Rock,
But where is the heart of Your people?
Where is Thy burning countenance?
Can it warm these cold hearts?
If You were not there firm in my soul,
I would create You.
But You are there—in the frigid heights,
On the mountain top, in the valley,
Even in the city that eats its young.

Yet I fear the weapons—
The button, the switchblade,

The boy with the semi-automatic rifle.
I fear these liars, these lost ones
Who lie in wait for me and my family.
Keep the knife from my wife's back,
And the backs of my children.
Let the Smiler in cloak pass us by.
Protect your servants who love you.
I search everywhere for truth and find confusion.
I am blinded by ashes in the wind,
Searching for Thee, O Rock,
In the desert and ocean of Los Angeles.

GOD BE WITH YOU

WENIGLIED
(For Rita)

Though these loved ones are not with us
But rather in us now, we mark their rest
With stone so we of the concrete world
Can see our memories more clearly
And perhaps consider with our hearts
The forces that brought us here,
Where we join hands in love
For these two dear remembered ones.
They are not bound by stone.
Though death has taken them from us—
We who are so poor in this century
      and death so rich.
Yet these two escaped the old world's nightmare
Of raids, pogroms, massacres.
They left the schtettel world of walls real and invisible
And came through pristine Vienna
To tough America, with its bustling metropols
Full of confusion and impossible hopes—
And they found new spirit to face old struggles.
Peddler Willy delivered bread and beautiful Tessie cooked;
They met and married, loved and fought,
And gave us three more children to love.
The joy of their youth is hidden from us
Behind a vast curtain we cannot penetrate.
It is of an era gone forever,
Hopefully with many sweet moments
In a century of blunt necessity and great cruelty.
The fight for bread and a roof took its toll,
But they struggled and succeeded.

They made their way, had full lives.
We owe them our devotion
Because they struggled well,
Struggled together in their need,
And they followed the essential commandments.

Love defeats death, but death will not die.
It lives beside us like a forgotten neighbor,
Who returns to stare quick at us
From a suddenly opened window.
Perhaps we grow accustomed to her stare;
Still, we don't invite her in for tea.
We miss them; I miss Willy's
"So, Bill. How's it goin'?" and
"Asher, whatcha doin'?"
And I will always remember
Tessie's eternal hunger to be loved.
I asked Willy once about his stay
In Vienna. He studied the clouds
Toward the airport, his glasses gold coins
In the evening sun, and he murmured,
"Vienna,... It all seems like a dream to me now...."
And his voice fell away, as they
Have now fallen away from our time together.
Their beautiful and cruel days are gone,
But that which we shared with them lives on.
They lie beneath this sunny green and these warm stones.
They do not embrace, but we can do that for them.
Perhaps they are dreaming now, together,
Without words, wherever lovers go

To finish their endless conversation.
Asher and Joshua have come among us
Not to replace them but perhaps
To ease our hearts a little. The light in
Tessie's eyes for her grandchildren
Will not die; it has passed into theirs.
We who remain will remember them,
And from time to time visit them
In our mind's eye, where they
Will pause, smile and wave to us
In old recognition and new understanding
Of certain possibilities we once shared.

12.13.92

DORA
(for Martin)

The unborn will measure us
And those gone on into light, like Dora,
Not by the strength needed to survive
The events that towered over her,
Or her ninety-year scamper
To land to land, city to city
Before square-toed death's advance.
It is not in being kind or even generous,
Though she was often that,
Not in the plain spun humor,
Not in her absolute dedication to family—
The endless meals prepared
For her son and his neighborhood friends—
Not in the friends she took into her care
(Though all this is somehow essential),
Not in the shawls and blankets she wove
To keep her hands knowledgeable.

It is rather in a certain quality of heart
That illuminates the lives of others
And shapes their vision of how women
And men can and should be in this world.
If I, even as a stranger, could know this,
Through her glance and touch,
How much moreso those of you
Who have known her for generations.

How do we honor those gone on
Like Dora? It is so hard to know
What is right now, in an age
When so much around us seems
To work against our trusting our feelings.
The simplest way to honor her
Is to look for her grace in ourselves
To seek those qualities she loved in others
And to treasure her descendants:
Those who already sweeten the earth,
Those she blessed with her arms—
Above all, the unborn who will soon cry out
For the love of a mother and grandmother.
Like children, we must go on
Reaching out, from day to day.

So, cold earth, take back
This little piece of you.
Time and Generations, cradle
This gentle Jewess in your arms,
As you cradled Rachel and Sarah.
But her heart you may not have.
Her heart stays here with us: deep
In her children, grandchildren,
Great-grandchildren, and everyone
Who knew the flow of her trust
And love through the rise,
Compromise and strife
Of this modern Jewish life.

Her shawls grace the life
    in our living rooms,
Her image hangs on our walls
    and nestles in our albums,
But she isn't in those things.

Let her be the dove of our imagination,
Let her be Spring to the cold fields
    where the world drives us.
Let her be the last thought before sleep,
    the last reason to weep.

9.5.93

You Don't Want to Know

I have no distinct memory of meeting Dora for the first time. She simply appeared on the sofa wherever there was a family gathering and I would be attracted to her settled, easy going qualities. Her self carried with it its own sense of place, and Dora's place was comfortable for me. We never spoke a great deal after I settled near her; it seemed enough to us that we were there, simply together. Sometimes she would hold my hand, not clinging or anxiously; and she surrendered me without a fuss to practically anyone. Whatever she saw in me, she could share with others. We came, in time, to kiss on the lips. Her kisses were dry and gentle, without a trace of a blunt need of attention, simply representing an unspoken intimacy, a gift experience had left her to bestow on those she chose.

In the first years together, neither of us chose to talk a lot. In the later years, she didn't feel much like it, or perhaps felt defeated by memory. During the in-between years, I attempted to record her version of the family history, and she had refused to say much. I mentioned the name of the town where she was raised. She looked at me curiously, as if to say, *You know this, and you're asking me?* Yes, they had owned land. No, she could not attend school. No, it was not pleasant. She did not react at all to key words: discrimination, pogrom, shoah. Finally, during the second attempt, I gave up and turned the tape recorder off. There was nothing on it really. Later, I recorded one of the final Beethoven string quartets on it with the idea of giving it to her. I never did, I forget why.

In the year before she died, we communicated very little. I was rushing from one project to the next. Sometimes I would simply settle into a chair near her at gatherings and touch her arm hello. Occasionally, it fell to me to fetch her for such gatherings. She always called me *Schweetheart* when I did this. I wish I'd done it more. She was saving her energy during this time, energy needed to deal with weakened limbs, the slight overweight her healthy appetite produced, and the inevitably increasing bouts of tiredness and lack of attentiveness. Still, her eyes brightened and deepened when she saw her great–grand-children, those who would replace her.

This past Thanksgiving, I glanced into the Horn's kitchen looking for Asher, who was hiding in another room as it turned out, and I saw an ashen presence, a shrunken waif huddled down in a great chair that had been pushed up close to the table. Even in her frailty, I had a strong sense of Dora's stubborn substantiality. Her sense of place was still intact. She did not see me; it was as if she were asleep with her eyes open. She was a sad and still center in the whirling atmosphere of our house. This was three months before her death. The next month, she came to our house for Hanukkah, and almost fell as she negotiated the curb of Stanley Avenue. A vast space had appeared between the car and our house. Once inside, she settled into our playroom, which is pretty much the center of activity in our house and did not move from there. Later, I observed a flushed but grim expression on her face, and went over and kissed her. She looked away from me with no recognition in her eyes. The days of recognition were pretty much past.

Gradually, it all became a burden, and she no longer

left her bed. When we left for Utah on January ninth, she was taking in little but beer. Fluid leaked from her knees and ankles. We stopped by when we returned ten days later and she recognized us individually, and seemed delighted that we were there. Her companions—her international community of friends, Yawapah from Thailand, Rosa from Mexico—took good care of her. All of this was arranged by Rita, of whom Dora once said to me, She is as good to me as a daughter.

Then, close to midnight on Friday, Jan. 22, Les was awakened by a phone call from her brother Michael. Dora had been gathered in as she slept. Hadn't we all said to ourselves, it would be a blessing if she could go peacefully? Les called Brian, with whom she had planned to visit Dora the next day. Now it would have to be enough to have been thinking of her. The last matriarch, the oldest pillar of the family had slipped away during sleep.

2

I knew Dora in the last decade of her life. That's not a very great span of time, and compared to that decade the actual time we spent together was minuscule. I knew her in the twilight years, in mid-winter, in slow-motion. Still, the petite woman filled my time and space as well as anyone ever has. Time and space, and Dora. Her spatial life during our years together evolved around two poles of activity: her two-room apartment in the Westside Apartment Building; and the house of her only son, Martin, and his wife Rita five blocks away. As those years progressed, she moved between those two axes of her spatial existence with decreasing frequency. She moved from a spry amble to a cautious, methodical plowing of an every-thickening atmosphere surrounding her, then to a cane-assisted, broken ramble, and finally to a walker. With the walker, autonomy ceased. More and more, she sat or napped, and moved and spoke less than anyone could remember. Then in the weeks before the midnight call came, she rose from bed unwillingly, asked only for beer, and lay smiling out from under the covers where she nursed her mild high and waited patiently to drift off into the sleep after sleep.

Leslie went over to her apartment after midnight to see Dora for the last time, before the UCLA team came to claim her body for the medical school. Her nurse had washed and made up so that she departed from her home composed and graceful in the mind of those who saw her leave. My wife said she looked very peaceful, even beautiful, her head resting lightly on the pillow. *My own mother's face had been childlike in the restful simplicity of its final sleep.*

She was, we thought, ready to let go. She was surrounded by people who really cared for her. She had always had a rich social life in her apartment building. The adjacent Westside Jewish Community Center offers a vital activity program for seniors. She regularly visited her great-grandchildren in the pre-school there. A circle of practiced caregivers orbited around her, lovingly making her days and nights as comfortable as was possible. She had the kind of steady soul that attracts loving care to it.

Her daughter-in-law and chief caregiver, Rita Horn, arranged in the mid-80s for a special birthday party for Dora in the Westside Apartments. Rob Lempert, a Harvard physicist, who has since drifted from my circle of

friends, and I presented a brief program of *Lieder* ––
Schubert, Schumann — in her honor. I have stored several
impressions from that night. I will put aside the dry
quality of the piano's tone, the slow tempi, and the
crowded conditions—the trained voice needs distance to
work—and concentrate on Dora. She sat beaming like a
queen ensconced on her cloth and wood throne, listening
carefully to the sounds dedicated to her. How many would
have such a concert given in their honor?

After the *Abendkoncert,* I approached Dora and kissed
her. She introduced me to a seemingly reserved lady
sitting nearby, who moaned to me as I took her hand,
Why Dora? she said, her eyes clinging to mine soulfully.
Bent over, still holding her hand, I glanced momentarily
into the lonely desert of self-pity that awaits a certain type
of person in old age, then retreated into politeness and
said, *She's the birthday girl!* Then I turned and winked at
Dora, who had been trying to cheer her dour friend up.
Dora rolled her eyes toward the ceiling with comic allure.
Why not for Dora? I said aloud. *It couldn't hurt,* said Dora
and offered me a piece of cake.

Dora didn't pity herself and didn't complain. When
questioned by a doctor, *Where does it hurt* and *How do you
feel* she would reply, *You're asking me?!* You had to observe
her to see what was going wrong; otherwise, you'd never
find out. The Doctor's asking *me* what's wrong? she would
say later, in understated outrage. She was not a squeaky
wheel, a kvetcher.

She was dutiful and generous. She married a man
who would also take her mother. She dedicated herself to
one child and deprived herself to help insure his success.
She took no credit when he succeeded, but enjoyed his

success enormously, for his sake. She was a calm, full spirit from the old world who strove and cared for others in their need, and she was cared for in her time of need.

I remember the strong impression that I got while singing to her: it seemed a natural and good thing to do. Her face smiled unceasingly as she lost herself in the music, in waking dream. It is clear in remembering that evening, that there was a balance and depth to her life that this music echoed. It was an experience that went far beyond that evening. Dora was living proof of the simple nature of nobility. To me, she is also proof of the ability of certain human qualities to transcend space and time.

3

Photographs *are* reductive. Photos slow, even stop time's flow in our comprehension of the time–space continuum enclosing us. The photographic process approximates the mind's act of constructing, then preserving visual images. A photo does this by accomplishing a visual simplification of image or person in situ. Such a simplification destroys the complexity of real context and allows dreamers like me to make–believe as we study photographs, to recreate scenes and color them with our sentiment. And even if I know this mimics the mind—is possibly even a lie of the mind—I enjoy this arresting of time. Time is our worst invention.

I especially love black and white photos in which I have to warm the hard–edged forms with memory and emotion. In the mental and emotional effort the illusion of suspended time is created. I love this illusion. In a world dominated by machines, this activity offers a chance to take the product of the machine age and, by exercising imagination and intuition in relation to it, to actually explore the effect of such inventions on the human self-image—and perhaps the soul. Imagination arrests time; intuition is a facility which ties us in a spatial, historical—topological—sense to the deepest roots of the birth of self.

I have a photo of Dora, but she is not alone in it. My son Asher's two-year-old countenance is pressed against hers. Even shadowed—everyone points out the photo's flaws, as if this mattered to the heart of my imagination—the two faces beam like twin suns from the cage of dots and lines forming but only vaguely representing and not at all enclosing their joy, their spirit. Two individuals, separated by nearly a century, form themselves joyfully, whole and complete, in my vision of this two-dimensional box.

It is around nine on a beautiful summer morning at Arrowhead. Dora had just finished her exercises, while Asher played nearby. I've shot the lake, Asher, and a nearby squirrel weaving its energy around a pine limb. I had given Dora her privacy earlier, but when she approached Asher and squatted beside him, studying his play with fallen leaves and acorns, I can no longer resist. I say, *How about a photo of you two?* Dora immediately says, *Okaaaay!* and grabs Asher to her. I barely get the camera to my eye before the shutter clicks and the moment of their instantaneous huddling has passed. I hadn't focused or really considered the composition. *Oh well*, I ask myself, *I wonder how it would have looked if I'd been ready?* Dora smooches Asher before she lets him go, and the day melts quickly about her into the other restful, stressful days of an Arrowhead retreat. Asher returns to his play,

77

Dora begins her daily knitting.

Later, I am amazed when I receive the prints from that day's shoot. In this particular photo, two lovely people, not at all separated by the eighty years between them, crush the raised cheeks of their faces together. They might be two beautiful children playing on a summer's day, children who paused then as Asher and Joshua occasionally do now, for a moment to share the spontaneous blessing of the other.

Such photographs are for me keys to the heart of memory. Pictures of the mind fade, along with the elasticity of the flesh; photos fade less quickly. Now that Dora has gone before us into that undiscovered country, I can only hold her so long in my mind, but Asher will have this photograph, this image of a summer's day he probably can not (and I will not) forget.

Dora didn't share my love of illusion, Her sturdy sense of self didn't need to take arms against a sea of metaphorical trouble; she let metaphors and time wash over her. She'd seen enough of the real thing. *Hamlet,* she said, *Who would want to read it? It's about a loser.* Dora was not a loser. She kept her <u>Complete Works of Shalom Aleichem</u> at hand. She had escaped the castle of horrors that mauled and swallowed the Yiddish Renaissance and she never looked back. *You don't want to know,* she said. And shrugged time off her sturdy shoulders, shoulders grown a little weaker in later years.

As I study this photo, I see its many imperfections: the shadows, the focus. Still, there is something of a miracle about it for me. Dora's eyes are focused on the camera—on me—dark and true. Asher, in a manner reminiscent of my mother, glances away, perhaps into the future. The pair of them live so clearly in my vision of this crude image. There is a power that defeats with inherent grace the technical difficulties in the execution of the taking of the photo, as well as the enormous disparity of age between the two subjects of the photo. That power emanates from strength of heart and steadfastness of soul. My hope to see my sons develop this power is as clear in my mind as the fact that Dora possessed it.

4.

Pouring over photographs, reductive clues to a wonderfully complex life story, a story full of mysteries — like the mysterious woman who appears in so many of the New York photos: who was she and what role did she play in Dora's life? There are vast portions of every life veiled in mystery. And we do somehow long to know the details of that life, even the dark details, not matter how terrible we sense or know them to have been. These are the historical hallways we will not stride or waltz down ourselves, yet they are somehow a part of our personal past. Wanting to know about them is like longing to find about a long-lost part of ourselves. There were complex forces that shaped the calm, petite figure who was such an important part of our lives. She was a source, a flower of the ancient, noble tree of Ruth and Esther. And she represented those who did not escape the jaws of death in Russian and Polish pogroms and the Nazi death camps in Europe and did not come to America to continue their family's life. And she did not want to be a Pandora for that family. She wouldn't open the box of her past. Perhaps she felt enough people had done that already. *You don't want to know.*

Dora created our present time. She is the mother of my second father, the grandmother of my wife, the great-grandmother of our children. We will live on in the present she created, in our vision of that present. She also was herself a spirit of the present. *You don't want to know* was her way of saying, *Live now, enjoy this time.*

As a writer, I create and work in the eternal present. This is the mode of the creator. With each individual reader, a situation is recreated, every word uttered for the first time, every glance burns, every stroke gleams. This is the world in which Dora now resides for me, somewhere between dream and reality, in the soul of the imagination. I know these images of Dora will fade from my memory, but I will cling to them, for the artifice they offer will be more real than anything else I have. Images of Dora in time, even the limited time we shared, are powerful in my personal myth: the family gatherings, the concert, the Arrowhead photograph, the smattering of remarks that color my personal dictionary with their sweet plainness. All these were Dora in Time, and the Space she occupies within me is very large and full of solid joy.

2.2.93